Animals in Action

Happy House

About Wise & Wide

- A systematic 6-level English reading program based on Lexile® measures
- Diverse and interesting topics chosen from the elementary curriculums of Korea and English speaking western countries
- Well-written books in various forms including fiction stories, descriptive texts, and classics retold
- The informative but original fiction stories grab your interest, leading to the easy and clear understanding of the educational content.
- Improve thinking skills with solid after-reading activities at all levels of the series.

Wise & Wide is a 6-level English reading program that consists of 60 books and each level is systematically divided by Lexile® measures. The Lexile® Framework for Reading is the most popular reading measuring system in American formal education curriculums and many English programs. Over 20 out of 50 states in the U.S. mark Lexile® measures directly on students' final report cards and over 300 well-known publishers adopt and use Lexile® measures.

Experience many kinds of readings written by professional writers from the U.S. and England. They used interesting topics that were carefully chosen after analyzing elementary curriculums from around the world including Korea, the U.S., England, and Australia among many others. Comprehensive after-reading activities including graphic organizers, speaking tasks, and After-reading Tests are ready for you.

Levels in the series and their corresponding Lexile® measures

Level	Lexile® measures	U.S. Grade
Level 1	Below 200L	Pre K - K
Level 2	190L - 400L	Lower Grade 1
Level 3	350L - 530L	Upper Grade 1
Level 4	420L - 650L	Grade 2
Level 5	520L - 940L	Grade 3 - 4
Level 6	830L - 1070L	Grade 5 - 6

* Smart Readers: Wise & Wide level 1 is applicable to the preschool level in the U.S.

* The source of the relationship between Lexile® measures and U.S. school grades: CCSS(Common Core State Standards) FOR ENGLISH LANGUAGE ARTS, APPENDIX A (2012, which is used by 45 states in the U.S.)

Topic List

	Level 1	Level 2	Level 3	Level 4	Level 5	Level 6
Book 1	Science>Biology: The hibernation of animals Story	Science>Biology: Living and nonliving things Story	Science>Biology: Animals & the Environment: Sea otters Story	Environment> Living with nature: The diver & the persimmon tree Story	Science>Biology> Animal: Amazing animals of the Amazon Story	Science>Biology: Germs, transmitted diseases Story
Book 2	Literature> World classics: Aesop's fables Story	Literature> Traditional fairy tale: Old tales about stones Story	Social Studies> Economy: To run a business to make and save money Story	Science>Biology> Plants: Photosynthesis Story	Science>Earth science: Earth's layers, earthquakes, volcanoes, and earth's atmosphere Report	Mathematics> Sequence: The golden ratio & the Fibonacci sequence Story
Book 3	Science>Physics: How shadows are formed Story	Literature> World classics: Peter Pan Story	Science>Scientific technology: Nanobots Story	Literature>Myths: World's creation stories Story	Literature> Legend: The story of King Arthur Story	Literature>Myths: Constellation myths Story
Book 4	Literature> Traditional literature: The Talmud Story	Science>Biology> Animal: Polar bears Story	Science>Biology> Animal: Mountain gorillas Story	Social Studies> Cultural anthropology: Amazing ancient cultures of the world Story	Science> Earth science: Clouds and weather Story	Literature> Human & animals: The friendship between a girl and a horse Story
Book 5	Social Studies> Ethics: Rules in daily life Story	Science>Biology: The five senses Report	Social Studies> Cultural anthropology: Astonishing festivals Report	Art>Music: Stories from two operas Story	Social Studies> World culture & history: The Renaissance Story	Sports> Board sports: Surfing & snowboarding Story
Book 6	Social Studies> World geography & travel: Tourist attractions around the world Story	Science>Biology> Animal: Dinosaurs Story	Science> Astronomy: The solar system Story	Social Studies> People: Three great people who overcame hardships Story	Science>Scientific technology: The wonderful world of robots Report	Art>Music: Composers of the Romantic Era Report
Book 7	Science> Space science: The life of astronauts Report	Social Studies> Cultural anthropology: Mythological monsters from around the world Report	Mathematics> Elementary mathematics: Numbers, measurement, shapes and data Report	Science & Social Studies> Technology & culture: Inventions from around the world Report	Art>Works of art: Famous paintings Report	Social Studies> Human & animals: Animals in action for human Report
Book 8	Social Studies> Cultural anthropology: Various living cultures of the world Story	Art>Music: Instruments in the orchestra Story	Social Studies> Life safety: Learning and using outdoor survival skills Story	Social Studies> History: The California Gold Rush Report	Social Studies & Science> Psychology: Psychology in everyday life Story	Literature> World classics: The Merchant of Venice Story
Book 9	Social Studies> Jobs: Interviews about jobs Report	Science>Scientific technology: Developments in technology in different times Story	Social Studies> Politics>Election: Running for 3rd grade class president Story	Literature> World classics: Stories of Sherlock Holmes Story	Literature> World classics: Adrift in the Pacific Story	
Book 10		Sports>Winter sports: Various aspects of some Winter Olympic sports Report				

* 10 books in each level will be published.

How to Use This Book

• Before Reading

You can easily find the topic and what kind of story you are about to read.

• The text

All the stories were written by professional writers from the U.S. and England, so you will read authentic and appropriate English sentences and expressions in every book in the series.

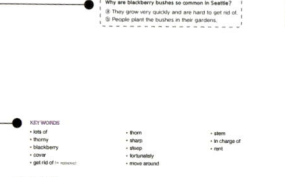

• Pop Quiz

Check out right away if you understand what you have just read by solving a pop quiz that checks your comprehension.

• Key Words

The key words and expressions on each page are listed for you to easily study them.

• Aha! Tips

Download free Korean explanations at *www.ihappyhouse.co.kr* for all of the sentences marked with "Aha!". These explain cultural, scientific, and economic knowledge or they deal with aspects of English such as grammatical structures or idiomatic expressions. There are lots of "Aha! Tips" to help you understand the text.

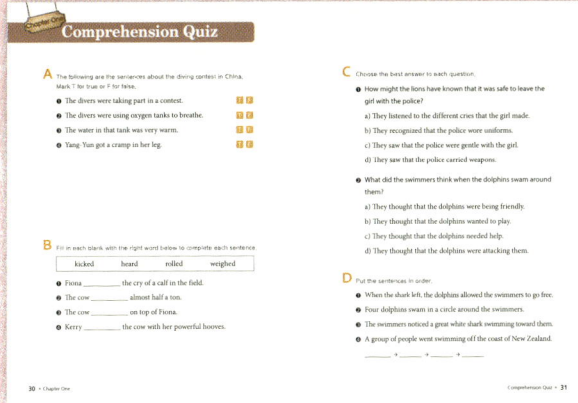

•Comprehension Quiz

After reading one chapter, solve various questions to find out if you fully understand the content.

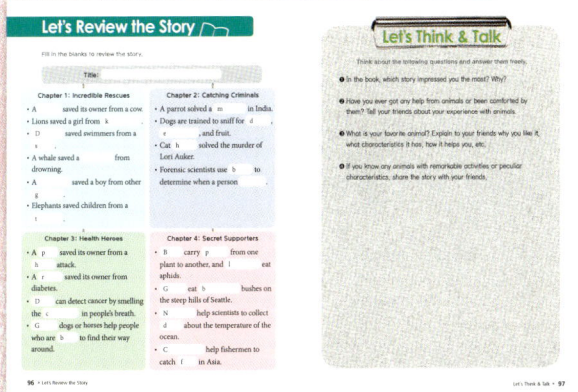

•Let's Review the Story /
•Let's Think & Talk

Fill in the blanks in the organizer to summarize the whole story. Express your own thinking and feelings about the story by answering the questions. You can build up logic and reasoning skills for your essay examinations in the future.

Appendix

Audio CD
In the CD audio book form, the texts are read vividly by American professional voice actors.
(MP3 files downloaded for free)

After-reading Test
Solve an additionally provided After-reading Test for each book.

The Korean translation, Answer Keys, a Word Quiz, a Word List, and Aha! Tips for each book
You can download them for free at *www.ihappyhouse.co.kr* or *www.darakwon.co.kr*

Before Reading

Animals in Action

Level 6–7,
Lexile®970L

•Social Studies〉Human & Animals
•Report

Animals that help humans with their remarkable activities

When you feed or bathe your pets while raising them, you might feel that animals need humans and get humans' help all the time. But that isn't true. Humans and animals have helped each other since ancient times. It was animals that played a big role when humans began farming and needed heavy things to be carried. In addition, in all countries of the world, there have been many stories about animals that fight against enemies attacking their masters or help their masters who have collapsed. Besides, there are a good number of animals that play a big role helping humans with various kinds of work. Therefore, it is not too much to say that humans and animals make history together.

Summary

There are some amazing cases in which animals saved humans such as a puppy that fought against a snake when the snake attacked a baby, a pig that brought a person to help by lying on the highway when its master collapsed with a heart attack, a dolphin that saved a diver who got a leg cramp, etc.

Especially, dogs provide various kinds of help to humans. They are guiding eyes for the blind and guiding ears for the deaf. In addition, pet dogs are best friends with autistic children or lonely people who have trouble making friends. Furthermore, their amazing sense of smell can notice what particular disease a person has and can also be used for catching criminals and detecting explosives.

Apart from dogs, African pouched rats are used for finding mines, and narwhals help us measure the temperature of the deep sea.

Shall we look closely into animals' remarkable activities?

Contents

Animals in Action

Animals in Action

Chapter One

Incredible Rescues

In the news, we hear stories of courageous people who rescue others from dangerous situations. Police officers, firefighters, paramedics, soldiers and many ordinary people risk their

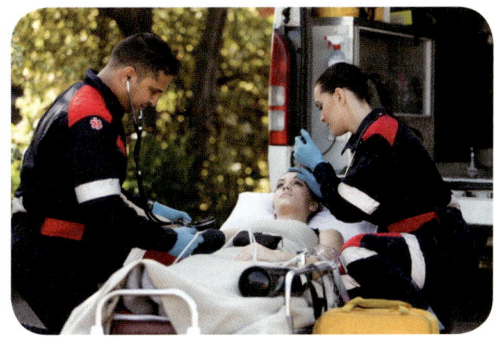

▲ paramedics

lives to save others. 🌐 But what about when that hero is an animal? Here are some amazing stories of heroic horses, daring dolphins, and other amazing animals that have rescued humans from dangerous situations. Some of them are loyal pets, trying to protect their owners. But even more incredible are the stories of wild animals that help humans.

KEY WORDS

- incredible
- rescue
- courageous (= brave)
- situation
- paramedic
- ordinary

- risk one's life
- save
- what about ~?
- amazing
- heroic
- daring

- loyal
- protect
- owner
- wild

You don't have to be big to be a hero! A Chihuahua is a tiny breed of dog that weighs less than 3 kg. But one Chihuahua named Zoey showed courage beyond her size when she defended her owner's grandson from a deadly rattlesnake. One-year-old Booker West was playing with water outside his grandparents' house in Masonville Colorado, U.S.A.

A rattlesnake – known for its powerful venom – slithered up behind him as he was playing.

Zoey put herself between the snake and the boy. She gave a series of high-pitched barks to call for help. Booker's grandfather, Monty Long, heard the barks and came to help, but the snake bit Zoey. A small amount of rattlesnake venom is enough to kill a tiny dog easily. Vets thought that the little dog would die. But Zoey's courage pulled her through and she survived the attack.

KEY WORDS

- Chihuahua
- tiny
- breed
- weigh
- courage
- beyond
- defend
- deadly

- rattlesnake
- known for
- venom (= poison)
- slither
- a series of
- high-pitched
- bark
- call (out) for help

- bite (bite-bit-bitten)
- amount (= quantity)
- enough
- vet (= veterinarian)
- pull through
- survive
- attack

Another dog, this time in Poland, saved the life of a three-year-old girl who wandered away from her home in freezing temperatures. The girl, whose name is Julia, spent the morning playing in the backyard of her home with her black dog. Then, she and the dog went exploring, but they got lost. They spent the night wandering around in the forest near Julia's home, while more than 200 people searched for them. As the temperature fell below freezing, Julia grew tired and very cold, and lay down to sleep.

If she had been alone, she would certainly have died of hypothermia. 📖 But her faithful dog lay next to her and kept her warm with its body heat.

Aha!

In the morning, Julia woke up and began to cry, and a firefighter heard her cries. He found the girl and the dog curled up together. Julia was taken to the hospital with frostbite, but everyone agreed that the dog had certainly saved her life.

KEY WORDS

- wander
- freezing
- temperature
- spend (spend-spent-spent)
- backyard
- go exploring (go-went-gone)
- get lost (get-got-gotten/got)
- search for (cf. search)
- below freezing
- grow (grow-grew-grown)
- tired

- lie down (lie-lay-lain)
- certainly
- die of
- hypothermia
- faithful (= loyal)
- next to
- keep (keep-kept-kept)
- body heat
- curl up
- frostbite

Many people know that dogs are loyal and will protect their owners, but here is a story of a horse doing the same thing. This story took place on a farm in Scotland, where a herd of cows was grazing.

Cows can be quite aggressive toward people who walk through fields where they are kept. These big creatures are very strong and powerful when they are angry.

Fiona Boyd lived on the farm, and when she heard the cry of a calf in the field, she went to see what was wrong. The mother cow thought that Fiona was coming to harm the calf, so she charged at Fiona.

POP QUIZ

Why did Fiona Boyd go into the field?

ⓐ She heard a calf crying.
ⓑ She heard a horse neighing.

KEY WORDS

- **take place** (take-took-taken) (*cf.* place)
- **a herd of**
- **graze**
- **quite**
- **aggressive**
- **creature**
- **calf**
- **harm**
- **charge at**
- **slam into**
- **knock**
- **roll**

- **rescuer**
- **race**
- **hooves**
- **leave ~ alone** (leave-left-left)
- **back away**
- **despite**
- **injury**
- **manage to** + *Verb*
- **crawl**
- **electric**
- **fence**

The cow, which weighed almost half a ton, slammed into Fiona several times. It knocked her to the ground and then rolled on top of her. This time it was Fiona who was crying out for help, and her rescuer was already in the field!

Fiona's horse, Kerry, heard the cries and raced over to help. Kerry kicked the cow with her powerful hooves until the cow left Fiona alone and backed away. Despite her injuries, Fiona managed to crawl several meters and roll under an electric fence, where she was safe from the cow.

Perhaps it's not surprising that domestic animals will protect their owners in situations of danger. After all, there may be a strong emotional bond between an owner and their pet.

But sometimes even wild animals will protect a human rather than ignoring them or even attacking them.

In Kenya, a twelve-year-old girl was kidnapped by three men who wanted to force her to marry one of them. She was missing for a week, but when the police finally found her, they were surprised to discover that she was unharmed.

Not only that, but she was being guarded by three lions.

They had scared away her kidnappers and had been making sure that nothing else came near her. When the police arrived, however, the lions moved away into the bush and disappeared. How did the lions know that the girl would be safe with the policemen but not with the other men? Nobody knows the answer to that, although the police think that it may have something to do with the girl's cries.

Perhaps the sounds that she made when she was distressed sounded like a lion cub calling for help. When she was rescued, her cries sounded different as she cried with relief. Perhaps the lions could tell the difference between the cries.

KEY WORDS

- perhaps
- domestic animal (cf. domestic)
- after all
- emotional
- bond
- rather than
- ignore
- kidnap
- force A to + Verb
- marry
- missing
- finally
- discover
- unharmed
- not only A(,) but (also) B

- guard
- scare away
- kidnapper
- make sure (make-made-made)
- however
- bush
- disappear
- although
- have something to do with (have-had-had)
- distressed
- sound like
- cub
- with relief
- tell the difference between (tell-told-told)

Dolphins are one of the most intelligent sea mammals. There are many stories of them helping people who are lost in boats to find their way home. But what about when the people are swimming in the water? People who swim with dolphins often say that they are playful and friendly, but sometimes they can be aggressive, especially if they have babies with them.

In 2004, a group of people were swimming in the sea near New Zealand when they were surrounded by four dolphins.

The dolphins swam in a circle around the four swimmers, and were acting so strangely that the swimmers thought that they were being attacked.

But they soon realized that a huge great white shark was coming closer and closer to them, swimming towards them at great speed.

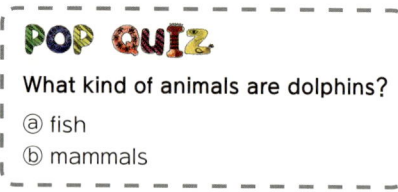

POP QUIZ

What kind of animals are dolphins?
ⓐ fish
ⓑ mammals

KEY WORDS

- intelligent
- mammal
- playful
- especially

- surround
- in a circle
- so ... that ~
- strangely

- realize
- great white shark
- at great speed

The dolphins were actually protecting the swimmers, keeping the shark away. The swimmers and the dolphins had to stay in this position for 40 minutes until the shark swam away. Then, the dolphins allowed the swimmers to go free so that they could swim, terrified, to the shore.

Dolphins are not the only intelligent sea mammals to understand when a human is in danger.

At an aquarium in China, several divers took part in a diving contest. They were free diving, which means that they were diving without oxygen tanks. They relied on the air in their lungs to keep them alive. The water in the tank was several meters deep, and was a similar temperature to the Arctic Ocean, which can be close to freezing.

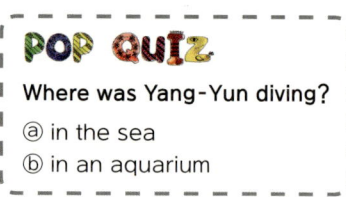

POP QUIZ

Where was Yang-Yun diving?
ⓐ in the sea
ⓑ in an aquarium

KEY WORDS

- actually
- position
- allow A to + *Verb*
- go free
- terrified
- shore
- in danger (↔ out of danger)
- aquarium
- diver
- take part in (= participate in)

- diving
- mean (mean-meant-meant)
- oxygen
- tank
- rely on
- lung
- alive
- similar
- the Arctic Ocean (*cf.* the Antarctic Ocean)
- be close to

A 26-year-old woman called Yang-Yun was one of the divers taking part in the contest. She dived all the way down to the bottom of the tank, but then she got a cramp in her leg. Her muscles wouldn't work properly, and she couldn't swim. She began to panic, and then to choke, taking in some water in her struggle to breathe.

KEY WORDS

- all the way (down) to
- bottom
- cramp
- muscle
- properly

- panic (panic - panicked - panicked)
- choke
- take in
- struggle
- breathe

Luckily for Yang-Yun, there were two beluga whales living in the tank. One of them noticed that she was having difficulty and swam over to help her. The whale took hold of Yang-Yun's leg in its mouth and began to push her toward the surface of the water.

Without the actions of this whale, Yang-Yun would certainly have drowned. The prize for the diving contest was to become a whale trainer at the aquarium. These whales are so intelligent that perhaps they should be training the divers instead!

Male gorillas are known for their great strength, and they can be very aggressive. They may grow as tall as a man, and are often much heavier than an adult human. So when a five-year-old boy called Levan Merritt fell into the gorilla enclosure at Jersey Zoo on Jersey, an island in the English Channel, things looked bad for him. His helpless parents and other visitors watched as he fell several feet onto a concrete floor and lay unconscious. Several gorillas came close to investigate, but even that was dangerous. A curious gorilla can easily hurt a child without meaning to.

POP QUIZ

What was the prize for winning the diving contest?

ⓐ a medal
ⓑ a job

KEY WORDS

- beluga whale
- notice
- have difficulty
- take hold of
- surface
- drown
- trainer
- train

- instead
- male
- strength
- as tall as
- adult
- enclosure
- channel
- things

- helpless
- concrete
- unconscious
- investigate
- curious
- hurt
- mean to + *Verb*

The male gorilla, Jambo, was the leader of the group. He placed himself between the injured boy and the rest of the gorillas. When other gorillas came close and acted in an aggressive way, Jambo chased them away.

Eventually, two brave zookeepers and a paramedic managed to reach Levan. He was taken to the hospital, where he made a full recovery from his injuries.

In 2004, there was an earthquake in the Indian Ocean. It caused a huge tsunami, which washed ashore in Phuket, Thailand. Many people were killed in the crashing wave as it rushed over the land, but one eight-year-old English girl called Amber was very lucky. She was riding on the back of an elephant called Ningnong. Ningnong raced up the shore as the water rose, breaking the force of the wave with her body. Amber stayed safely above the water and out of danger.

Ningnong was not the only elephant who protected children that day. Another elephant had been brought to the beach to entertain tourists. It carried several small children to safety on its back when the wave struck.

POP QUIZ

Why was the second elephant brought to the beach?
ⓐ to carry luggage to the hotels
ⓑ to entertain tourists

KEY WORDS

- place oneself
- injured
- the rest of
- chase away
- eventually
- zookeeper
- make a (full) recovery
- earthquake

- the Indian Ocean
- cause
- tsunami
- wash
- ashore
- crash
- rush
- land

- **rise** (rise-rose-risen)
- **bring** (bring-brought-brought)
- **entertain**
- **tourist**
- **carry**
- **safety**
- **strike** (strike-struck-struck/stricken)

The same earthquake caused a tsunami along the coast of India, too. A seven-year-old boy there was saved by his family's dog. When the wave approached, most of the family ran uphill to get away from it.

But the boy panicked and ran into a concrete hut close to the beach. The dog ran into the hut and grabbed the boy by the collar of his shirt. The dog dragged the boy outside and then it nipped at the boy's heels and nudged him to make him run up the hill, away from the huge wave.

In all these cases, animals saved people's lives, proving that they can show the same courage and compassion as humans.

POP QUIZ

Why did the dog nip at the boy's heels?

ⓐ to make him run up the hill
ⓑ to make him go into the hut

KEY WORDS

- coast
- approach
- uphill
- get away from
- hut

- grab
- collar
- drag
- nip at
- heel

- nudge
- case
- prove
- compassion

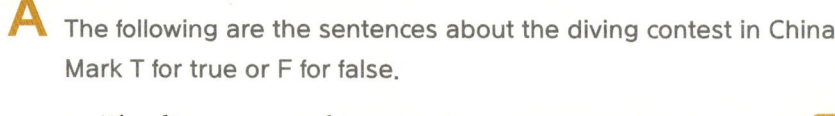

Comprehension Quiz

A The following are the sentences about the diving contest in China. Mark T for true or F for false.

➊ The divers were taking part in a contest. T F

➋ The divers were using oxygen tanks to breathe. T F

➌ The water in that tank was very warm. T F

➍ Yang-Yun got a cramp in her leg. T F

B Fill in each blank with the right word below to complete each sentence.

kicked	heard	rolled	weighed

➊ Fiona _____ the cry of a calf in the field.

➋ The cow _____ almost half a ton.

➌ The cow _____ on top of Fiona.

➍ Kerry _____ the cow with her powerful hooves.

C Choose the best answer to each question.

❶ How might the lions have known that it was safe to leave the girl with the police?

a) They listened to the different cries that the girl made.

b) They recognized that the police wore uniforms.

c) They saw that the police were gentle with the girl.

d) They saw that the police carried weapons.

❷ What did the swimmers think when the dolphins swam around them?

a) They thought that the dolphins were being friendly.

b) They thought that the dolphins wanted to play.

c) They thought that the dolphins needed help.

d) They thought that the dolphins were attacking them.

D Put the sentences in order.

❶ When the shark left, the dolphins allowed the swimmers to go free.

❷ Four dolphins swam in a circle around the swimmers.

❸ The swimmers noticed a great white shark swimming toward them.

❹ A group of people went swimming off the coast of New Zealand.

_____ → _____ → _____ → _____

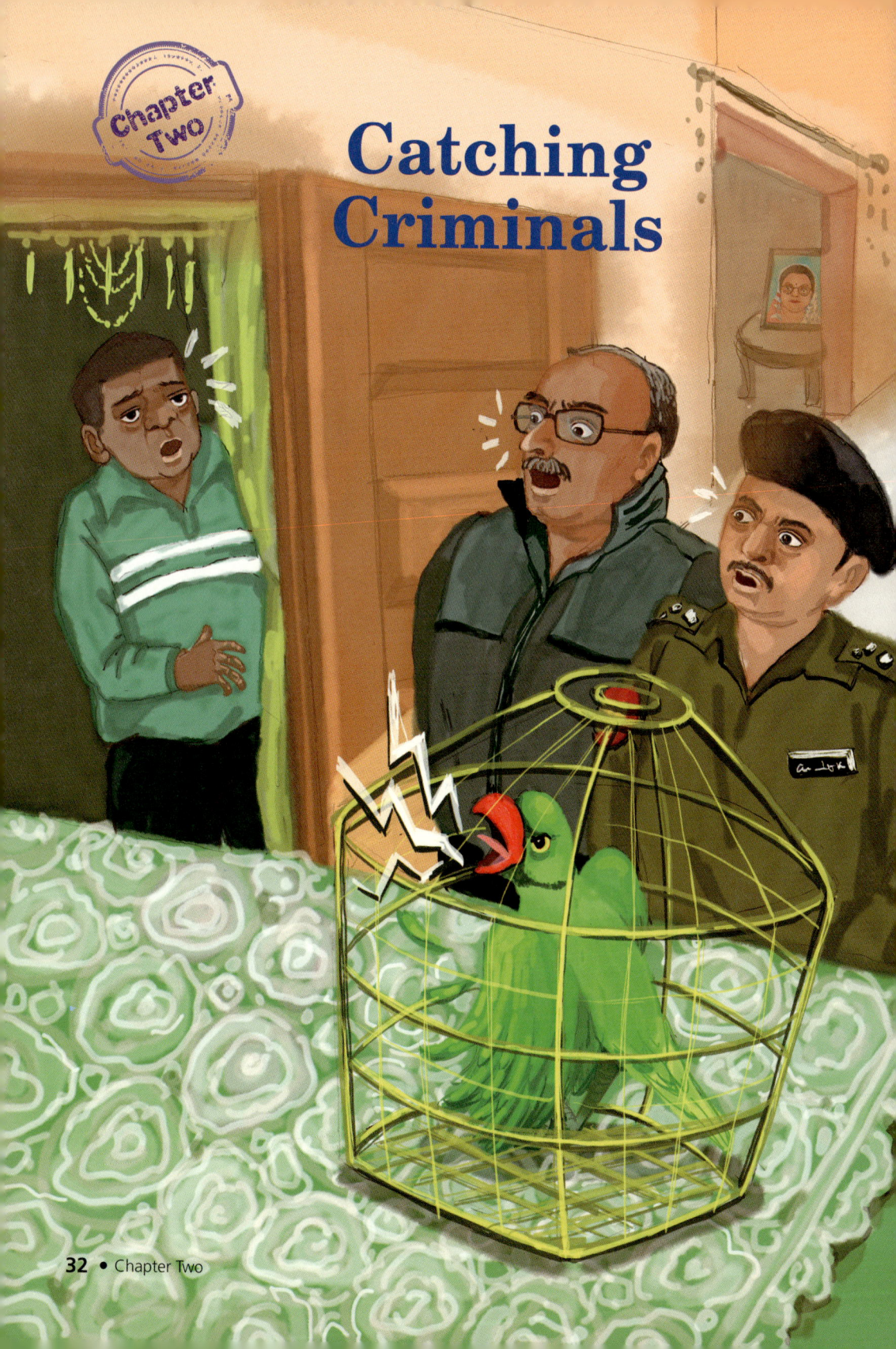

Catching Criminals

When crimes are committed, the police are called in to solve them and to catch the criminals. But sometimes the police officers need extra help, and it can come from surprising sources!

In 2014, in India, a 45-year-old woman called Neelam Sharma was murdered, and her pet dog was also killed. For a whole week, police officers and detectives tried to find out what had happened. But they had no idea who had committed the crime. Neelam's husband, Vijay, remained at his home with his parrot, Hercule, while the police investigated. His nephew, Ashutosh, visited them at the house during this time. But Vijay noticed that each time Ashutosh visited, the parrot behaved strangely. It screeched loudly each time it saw Ashutosh, or when his name was mentioned by family members. Vijay became suspicious and told the police about the parrot's strange behavior.

KEY WORDS

- criminal
- crime
- commit
- call ~ in
- solve
- extra

- source
- murder
- detective
- find out (find-found-found)
- have no idea
- remain

- nephew
- behave
- screech
- mention
- suspicious
- behavior

The police checked details of phone calls that Ashutosh had made, and decided to question him about the murder. Ashutosh confessed that he had gone to Neelam's house in order to steal money from her. Although he disguised himself, he was worried that Neelam might recognize him, so he killed her. When her pet dog began barking, he killed the dog as well, but he didn't notice the parrot watching him.

The parrot's name, Hercule, is the same as the name of a famous fictional detective. Hercule Poirot is a detective in books by author Agatha Christie. It seems that this parrot wanted to be a famous detective, too!

Dogs are often used by police officers for tasks that cannot be carried out by a human. Their loyal nature and courage make them ideal companions for human police officers, but they also bring special skills and senses. Due to their great sense of smell, dogs can detect drugs, explosives, or other forbidden substances.

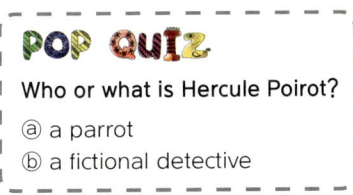

POP QUIZ
Who or what is Hercule Poirot?
ⓐ a parrot
ⓑ a fictional detective

KEY WORDS

- check
- detail
- make a phone call
- question
- confess
- in order to + *Verb*
- steal (steal-stole-stolen)
- disguise oneself
- recognize

- as well
- fictional
- Agatha Christie
- task
- carry out
- nature
- ideal
- companion
- sense

- due to
- detect
- drug
- explosive
- forbidden (*cf.* forbid(forbid-forbade/forbad-forbidden/forbid))
- substance

At Australian airports, for example, dogs are trained to sniff the bags of people arriving in the country to make sure that they are not carrying fruit. The fruit industry is very important in Australia. Fruit from other countries may bring diseases or pests into the country which can harm Australian fruit trees. The dogs and their handlers walk around the baggage claim area. If the dogs sniff forbidden food, they sit down by the bag. The handler then questions the traveler and searches the bag.

Some dogs are specially trained to detect explosives or bombs. They, too, may be used at airports or any other place where police suspect explosives may be. Other dogs are specially trained to detect drugs. The training is fun for the dogs so that they enjoy their work.

KEY WORDS

- sniff
- disease
- pest
- handler (*cf.* handle)
- baggage claim (**area**) (*cf.* area)
- traveler
- specially
- bomb
- suspect

Usually, a dog trainer begins a dog's training by playing a game with the dog using a towel. The dog likes to bite on one end of the towel so the trainer holds onto the other end, and they both try to pull it away from each other. The dog enjoys this game of "tug-of-war" very much. Then, the trainer puts a bag of drugs inside the towel so that the dog can smell it while the game is taking place. After a while, the dog thinks that the smell of the drugs is the smell of the towel.

POP QUIZ

What do the dogs do if they detect fruit in a traveler's bag?

ⓐ They sit down by the bag.
ⓑ They bark loudly.

KEY WORDS

▪ **hold onto** (hold-held-held)   ▪ **tug-of-war**   ▪ **after a while**

In the next stage of training, the trainer hides the towel, with the drugs inside it, in different places. The dog sniffs around, trying to find its favorite toy. It scratches or digs excitedly when it finds the smell. During the training, its reward is another game of "tug-of-war" with the towel! This method can be used to train dogs to detect drugs with different smells.

KEY WORDS

- stage
- hide (hide-hid-hidden)
- scratch
- dig (dig-dug-dug)
- excitedly
- reward
- method
- device
- explode

▲ a police dog that sniffs to check if there are any drugs or explosives in the bag

The same method is used (with explosives inside the towel) to train dogs to find explosives. This time, they are trained to sit down when they find it. Scratching at an explosive device may cause it to explode and hurt or kill any dogs and humans in the area.  Instead, they sit down and look at their handler to show that they have found something.

POP QUIZ

What do the dogs do if they detect explosives?

ⓐ They scratch the explosives.

ⓑ They sit down and look at their handler.

Another important use of the dog's great sense of smell is in tracking humans. If a person has gone missing, or is on the run from the police, dogs may be used to find them. The dog is given something to sniff that belongs to the missing person. Then, it follows the person's scent trail to track him or her down. Many criminals who thought that they were safely hidden have been found by police sniffer dogs.

Other police dogs are trained to use their sense of smell in order to find cadavers. This may be important in solving a crime, but it is also very useful when a disaster, such as an earthquake, has occurred. In these cases, dogs can find living people as well as dead ones, and may save many lives.

POP QUIZ

How do police dogs find missing people?
ⓐ by following footprints left by the person
ⓑ by following a trail of the person's scent

KEY WORDS

- track
- go missing
- on the run
- belong to
- follow
- scent (= odor)
- trail
- sniffer dog

- cadaver (= dead body)
- disaster
- such as
- occur
- A as well as B
- keep order (cf. order)
- be faced with (cf. face)
- snarl

- run away
- chase after
- fasten
- affection
- form
- retire

Some police dogs are not used for their sense of smell, but to help keep order. If criminals are faced with snarling dogs, they will not usually try to run away. If they do, the dogs chase after them and holds them by fastening their teeth around their arms or legs.

Often, a strong bond of affection forms between the handler and the dog. When the dog retires from police work, the handler may keep it as a domestic pet.

Dogs are not the only animals with a good sense of smell that may be used to help in the fight against crime.

In the 1970s, gerbils were used at an airport in Israel to catch terrorists who might try to get onto an airplane. The gerbils' cages were placed near security checkpoints, which travelers had to pass through on their way to board their flight.

KEY WORDS

- **fight against** (fight-fought-fought)
- **gerbil**
- **terrorist**
- **cage**
- **security checkpoint**
- **pass through**
- **on one's way to**
- **board**

A fan blew air into the cage so that the gerbils could smell the odor coming from the travelers. The gerbils were trained to press a lever if they detected the odor of adrenaline in the air. Adrenaline is a chemical that is produced in the human body when a person is nervous or excited. It makes the heart beat faster and the palms sweat, and it prepares the body to fight or to run away. The people who tried this experiment with the gerbils thought that terrorists would be nervous when they came through the security checkpoint. They thought that the gerbils would detect this. The experiment worked, since the gerbils were good at detecting adrenaline in the air. But they could not tell the difference between a terrorist and someone who was simply afraid of flying, so the experiment was stopped.

POP QUIZ

What kind of animals were used in Israel to try to catch terrorists?

ⓐ dogs　　ⓑ gerbils

KEY WORDS

- **blow** (blow-blew-blown)
- odor
- press
- lever
- adrenaline
- chemical

- produce
- nervous
- **beat** (beat-beat-beaten)
- palm
- sweat
- prepare

- experiment
- since
- be good at
- be afraid of

Some unusual animals are very useful in helping to crack crimes, even though they don't know it! Forensic science is the scientific examination of tiny clues – such as hairs, footprints, fingerprints, blood, etc. – left behind at crime scenes. The hairs of pet cats stick to clothing, curtains, and furniture. They can be used to solve all kinds of crimes. For example, if a burglar breaks into a house where a cat lives, then cat hairs will stick to him or her. The police can then use these hairs as evidence to prove that the burglar was at the house.

Cat hairs have even been used to solve murder cases. In May 1989, an American woman named Lori Auker disappeared. Sadly, her dead body was found by police three weeks later, and they began to investigate the case. One of their suspects was Lori's husband, Robert. He had not lived with his wife for quite a long time. There were surveillance cameras near Lori's home, and police watched the footage. They noticed that Robert's car was often seen in the area. They became suspicious when Robert's parents said that he had recently cleaned the car, and then he had sold it.

POP QUIZ

How did the police know that Robert's car was often near his wife's home?

ⓐ They looked at footage from surveillance cameras.
ⓑ They found tire tracks near her home.

KEY WORDS

- unusual
- crack
- even though (= although)
- forensic science
- scientific
- examination
- clue
- footprint
- fingerprint

- leave behind
- crime scene
- stick to (stick-stuck-stuck)
- burglar
- break into (break-broke-broken)
- evidence
- surveillance
- footage
- recently

Amazingly, it was Lori's two cats which helped to solve the crime. Some cat hairs that were stuck to Lori's clothes came off when Robert put her body into his car. Police officers found the hairs in his car, so they knew that Lori had been there. This evidence helped to prove that Robert had murdered his wife.

It sounds horrible, but forensic scientists can use bugs to find out at what time a person died.  There are certain flies that quickly gather on the dead bodies of animals or humans. They lay their eggs on the cadaver, and a few hours later the insect larvae hatch from the eggs and crawl about. The larvae grow bigger, and at last they turn into adult flies, which fly away and leave the cadaver. When forensic scientists look closely at the larvae and measure how big they are, they can calculate the time of death.

KEY WORDS

- amazingly
- come off (come-came-come)
- horrible
- forensic scientist
- bug
- certain
- fly
- gather
- lay (one's) eggs (lay-laid-laid)

- insect
- larvae
- hatch
- at last
- turn into
- closely
- measure
- calculate

The police use other animals, too, though not always for solving crimes. Some police officers, called "mounted police", carry out their duties on horseback. In the UK, police horses are used when there is a large crowd that the police need to control. They are often seen at soccer matches where the crowd is large and excited. The horses are specially trained to be confident when there are loud noises such as sirens or people shouting.

Sitting on the back of the horse, a police officer can see everything that is going on. Also, people will move away from a large horse. Horses can travel easily where motor vehicles cannot. This means that horses are used by the police in some countries to patrol wilderness areas.

But members of Jordan's Royal Desert Forces patrol their areas not on horses but on camels! The camels are used to the harsh, sandy conditions. They are used for catching smugglers and recovering stolen cars from the rough terrain.

The Border Security Forces of India use a camel patrol, "Camel Cavalry." It watches over the international border between India and Pakistan.

POP QUIZ

What is special about "mounted police"?
ⓐ They ride on horses while they carry out their duties.
ⓑ They use dogs to catch criminals.

KEY WORDS

- mounted
- on horseback
- control
- match
- confident
- siren
- motor vehicle
- patrol
- wilderness
- Jordan

- royal
- desert
- force(s)
- camel
- harsh
- sandy
- conditions
- smuggler
- recover
- stolen

- rough
- terrain
- border
- security forces
  (*cf.* security)
- cavalry
- watch over
- international

Comprehension Quiz

A Complete the sentence by matching each animal's activity with the related country.

❶ A parrot solved a crime in   •   • a) Israel.

❷ Dogs sniff bags to detect fruit in   •   • b) Jordan.

❸ Gerbils were used to catch terrorists in •   • c) Australia.

❹ Camels are used to catch smugglers in   •   • d) India.

B Fill in each blank with the right word below to complete each sentence.

track	sniff	fastening	cadavers

❶ The dog is given something to _____ that belongs to the missing person.

❷ The dog follows the person's scent trail to _____ him or her down.

❸ Some dogs are trained to use their sense of smell to find

_____.

❹ A dog may hold criminals by _____ its teeth around their arms or legs.

C Choose the best answer to each question.

1 How did Hercule let people know that Ashutosh was the murderer?

a) Hercule stood in the place where the crime was committed.

b) Hercule spoke Ashutosh's name to the police.

c) Hercule found some money that Ashutosh had stolen.

d) Hercule behaved strangely whenever Ashutosh's name was mentioned.

2 Why do some police officers use horses to patrol wilderness areas?

a) The horses are not afraid of wild animals.

b) The horses are used to the harsh, sandy conditions.

c) The horses can travel long distances very quickly.

d) The horses can travel easily where motor vehicles cannot.

D Circle the right word for each underlined part.

1 The Border Security Forces of India use a (gerbil / parrot / camel) patrol.

2 Mounted police carry out their (duties / crimes / baggage) on horseback.

3 Forensic scientists use larvae to (complete / change / calculate) the time of death.

Health Heroes

The close bond between pets and their owners means that animals are the perfect helpers in everyday life. Pets are constant companions, so they may be present in the home when nobody else is. There are many stories of pets saving their owners' lives when they had a health emergency. Dogs are good at this, since they are loyal and easily trained, but sometimes more unusual animals are the heroes.

KEY WORDS

- helper
- constant
- present
- emergency
- heart attack
- property
- fence in
- highway
- gap
- traffic

A pig called Lulu lived with her owner, Jo Ann, in the U.S.A.
One day, Jo Ann had a heart attack, and lay unconscious on the
family property. Lulu noticed that something was wrong, but she
was in a yard that was fenced in. Nobody knows how, but Lulu
managed to open the gate and get out of the yard. Then, she
went to the nearest highway to find help.

This clever pig waited for a gap in the traffic. Then, she walked
out onto the middle of the highway and lay down!

At first, nobody stopped, and the drivers simply went around Lulu. Every now and again, she got up and went back to her home to check on Jo Ann. Each time, she went back to the highway and lay down again.

Luckily, a driver stopped to see why a huge pig was lying down on the highway. Lulu got up and led the driver back to her home, where Jo Ann was still unconscious. The driver called paramedics, who took Jo Ann to the hospital. She recovered from her heart attack and thanked Lulu by giving her a donut.

In England, a man called Simon Steggall fell asleep on his couch. At least, his wife thought that he was just asleep, so she left him in peace. However, Simon suffered from diabetes, an illness which meant that he could not control the level of sugar in his blood.  If the level of sugar was too high or too low, he became unconscious. Dory lived indoors and she somehow knew that something was wrong.

POP QUIZ

How did JoAnn thank Lulu for saving her life?

ⓐ JoAnn gave Lulu a medal.
ⓑ JoAnn gave Lulu a donut.

KEY WORDS

- at first
- (every) now and again
- **lead** (lead-led-led)
- **fall asleep** (fall-fell-fallen)
- couch

- at least
- leave ~ in peace
- suffer from
- diabetes
- illness

- level
- indoors
- somehow

First, she thumped her hind legs against the floor. This is a natural action that rabbits do to warn others of danger. Then, Dory jumped up onto the couch and began to lick Simon's lips to try to wake him up. Simon's wife noticed that Dory was behaving strangely. She, too, realized that something was wrong. She called the paramedics, who came to the house and took Simon to the hospital. Without Dory's actions, Simon could have died.

KEY WORDS

- thump
- hind leg
- natural
- warn
- lick

Some dogs are so good at detecting problems in people with diabetes that they can be used as health companions. Medical Assistance Diabetic Alert Dogs are specially trained to know when their owner's blood sugar level is incorrect. When a diabetic person's blood sugar level drops too low, his or her odor changes. A human can't detect this odor, but the sensitive nose of a dog can. The dog raises the alarm by barking or by licking the owner's face.

The sensitivity of dogs to different odors may also be used to detect cancer in humans. A study in 2003 used five dogs to sniff different samples of breath. Some of the samples were from healthy people and some were from people with cancer.

POP QUIZ

Why did Dory thump her hind legs against the floor?
ⓐ to warn others of danger
ⓑ to show others that she was angry

KEY WORDS

- medical
- assistance
- diabetic
- alert

- blood sugar level
- incorrect
- drop
- sensitive

- raise the alarm (cf. raise)
- sensitivity
- cancer
- breath

Human breath is not just made of air. It contains different gases, droplets of water, molecules of food or toothpaste, and chemicals that may be produced by bacteria. Scientists believe that cancer tumors release chemicals into the body.

The chemicals get into the breath, and dogs can smell them. Dogs can be helpful to people with other health problems, such as epilepsy. Epilepsy is a problem with the brain, which can cause people to have a seizure.

The person's body muscles may stiffen or jerk about. The person cannot control them, often because he or she is unconscious. The person may be injured or stop breathing. It is important

that someone is there to care for the person during the seizure and afterwards. Seizure dogs are helpful to a person with epilepsy, and are especially used to help children.

POP QUIZ

Which of these is something that often happens to people with epilepsy?

ⓐ seizures
ⓑ high blood sugar level

KEY WORDS

- be made of
- contain
- droplet
- molecule
- bacteria

- tumor
- release
- epilepsy
- have a seizure (*cf.* seizure)
- stiffen

- jerk
- care for (= take care of)
- afterwards

The dog's first task is to raise the alarm if a child is having a seizure, so that an adult can come to help the child. The dog may do this by barking. Sometimes, it presses a paw against a pedal, which sounds an alarm. Sometimes, a dog lies next to a child who is having a seizure so that the child is not injured. If children roll against a dog, they will be hurt less than if they roll into an item of furniture. Some dogs even seem able to detect a seizure before it happens.

Nobody knows how a dog does this. Perhaps it detects small movements or changes in the behavior of the child. Since the dog is ready, it can rush toward the child when a seizure begins. It can place itself so that the child falls onto the dog instead of onto the floor.

Other children may have a health problem with their thoughts and feelings rather than in their body.  Some children suffer from autism. This means that a child does not connect and join in with the world in the same way that other children do.

POP QUIZ

How might a seizure dog raise the alarm?

ⓐ by barking
ⓑ by wagging its tail

KEY WORDS

- paw
- pedal
- against

- item
- (be) able to + *Verb*
- be ready (to + *Verb*)

- autism
- connect with
- join in with

An autistic child will play with other children, but he or she may not be able to make friendships or to understand how other children feel. He or she may not talk much or

look at other people, and life is difficult and frightening for that child. Sometimes the child may not be able to control his or her behavior, and may have difficulty sleeping. All this is exhausting for both the child and the parents.

Experts have found that dogs are very helpful to families with autistic children. A dog does not mind if a child does not speak to it or look at it, or if the child stays awake all night.

KEY WORDS

- autistic
- make a friendship (*cf.* friendship)
- understand (understand-understood-understood)
- frightening
- exhausting
- expert
- mind
- stay awake

The presence of a friendly, loyal dog calms the child. It helps the child to sleep at night and to feel safe during the day. When it is time to play, the child can play with the dog and order it to carry out certain tasks. Another child would not like to be ordered about in this way, but the dog enjoys it as if it were a game.

KEY WORDS

- presence
- calm
- it is time to + *Verb*
- as if

There are many other types of assistance dogs, which help people with all kinds of health problems. People who are blind may have a guide dog, which helps its owner to walk about safely and to cross roads. People who are deaf may have a hearing assistance dog, which alerts its owner when someone is at the door or a baby is crying. People who cannot move about easily may have an assistance dog to help with daily tasks. The dog can pick up items from the floor, remove laundry from the washing machine, or even go to the local shop!

POP QUIZ

Who might be helped by a guide dog?

ⓐ someone who is deaf
ⓑ someone who is blind

The dog may wear a special jacket with pockets for money and a shopping list. The shop owner takes the correct money and gives the dog an item to carry home in its mouth. Assistance dogs must be carefully trained for a long time in order to carry out these tasks.

It is not only dogs that may be trained to help people in the home. Some people in the U.S.A have a miniature horse instead! The horses are especially helpful for blind people, and carry out the same duties as a guide dog. They guide their owners safely around, and are calm in crowds. They are also loyal and friendly toward their owners. Of course, an ordinary horse would not be a good animal to take into the house. But miniature horses are about the same height as a large dog.

KEY WORDS

- type
- blind
- guide dog
- walk about
- deaf
- daily
- pick up
- remove
- laundry
- local
- miniature horse (*cf.* miniature)
- height

Horses are especially suitable for owners who are allergic to dog hair. They are also good for people who are afraid of dogs. Also, a horse can live outside the house when it is not working.

▲ miniature horse

But many owners do allow their horses inside the house. They are trained to be clean and not to poop indoors!

Horses also live a lot longer than dogs do. This means that owners and horses can live together for many years. The average length of a horse's life is 30~40 years, instead of the 8~12 years that a dog lives.

Miniature horses must never be ridden, but they are strong enough to bear the weight of a person leaning on them. This can be useful if a person finds it difficult to get up out of a chair.

KEY WORDS

- suitable
- allergic to
- poop
- average
- length
- ride (ride-rode-ridden)
- bear (bear-bore-borne)
- lean on
- rider

A horse uses its natural behavior to help its owner. In the wild, if there is a blind horse in a herd, a horse that can see takes care of the blind horse. The horse that can see stays close to the blind horse and guides it around. In the same way, a miniature horse helps its owner who may be blind or have another health problem. There are also many stories of horses bringing injured riders back home to safety.

Even for healthy people, having pets can make them happier. Owning a dog means that the owner should go out with the dog to exercise it each day. It is a good way to meet other people, which may be important if the owner is lonely. Having another living thing in the home to care for can help humans to feel less lonely. When people stroke a pet such as a cat, dog, or rabbit, their blood pressure drops and they become more relaxed. When people are stressed or anxious, touching another living thing helps them to feel needed and loved.

Some charities take well-behaved cats and dogs to visit old or ill people, or into prisons and schools. The animals help people to recover from illness or to cope with difficult feelings. Having a pet is good for children, too. A child can learn how to feed and take care of an animal and to take responsibility for keeping it clean and healthy. Playing with pets helps children to relax, and many children talk to their pets. They may tell them things that they may not want to tell anyone else.

Scientists have found that playing with a pet produces chemicals in the blood that make people feel happy and calm. Some scientists also think that if children grow up with pets around the home, they are less likely to suffer from allergies and asthma. But it is important to remember that if a child already has asthma, getting a new pet may make it worse.

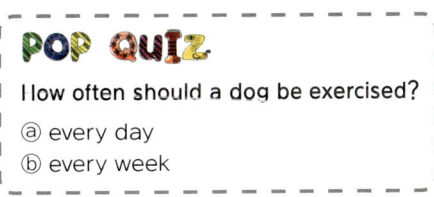

POP QUIZ

How often should a dog be exercised?
ⓐ every day
ⓑ every week

KEY WORDS

- exercise
- living thing
- stroke
- blood pressure
- relaxed
- anxious

- charity
- well-behaved
- prison
- cope with
- feed (feed-fed-fed)
- take responsibility for

- grow up
- be likely to + *Verb*
- allergy
- asthma

Comprehension Quiz

A Mark T for true or F for false.

❶ Dory went to Simon's wife and licked her.　T　F

❷ Dory lived in Simon's garden.　T　F

❸ Dory jumped up onto the couch to help Simon.　T　F

❹ Dory licked Simon's fingers to try to wake him.　T　F

B Fill in each blank with the right word below to complete each sentence.

odors	molecules	samples	tumors

❶ The sensitivity of dogs to _____ may be used to detect cancer in humans.

❷ Some of the breath _____ were from healthy people.

❸ Scientists believe that cancer _____ release chemicals into the body.

❹ Human breath may contain _____ of food.

C Choose the best answer to each question.

❶ Why are pets generally helpful to their owners in everyday life?

a) They can open doors and do jobs around the house.

b) They may be present in the home when nobody else is.

c) They can communicate with their owners better than people can.

d) They can do things that humans cannot do.

❷ How do some dogs know when a person's blood sugar level has dropped?

a) They taste the difference in the person's sweat.

b) They see the difference in the person's behavior.

c) They hear the difference in the person's voice.

d) They smell the difference in the person's odor.

D Put the sentences in order.

❶ Lulu lay down on the highway until a car stopped.

❷ A car driver followed Lulu home and got help for Jo Ann.

❸ Lulu's owner, Jo Ann, had a heart attack and became unconscious.

❹ Lulu managed to open the gate and get out of the yard.

_____ → _____ → _____ → _____

Secret Supporters

Managing the Environment

There are many ways in which animals support humans every day without people even noticing. They don't need our instructions to get on with their job; they go about it secretly and quietly. Insects take pollen from one plant to another, so that the plant will grow fruit and produce seeds. Without insects, such as bees, that do this, a lot of the foods that people eat would not exist!

Other animals help to control pests. Ladybugs, for example, eat tiny green insects called aphids, which can destroy important crops. All these things are part of nature, and help our planet to work as it is meant to.

KEY WORDS

- supporter
- manage
- environment
- support
- instruction
- get on with

- go about
- secretly
- pollen
- seed
- exist
- ladybug

- aphid
- destroy
- crop
- planet
- be meant to + *Verb*

Sometimes humans use animals' natural behavior to help them manage the environment. The city of Seattle, in the U.S.A, has lots of hills. Thorny blackberry bushes grow on the hills and quickly cover them. These plants grow quickly and soon cover large areas of land so that nobody can go there. They are difficult for humans to get rid of because the thorns are so sharp, and the hills are so steep. Fortunately, there is one animal that easily moves around on steep hills, and also loves to eat thorny blackberry stems. The people in charge of the city rent sixty goats to eat the blackberry bushes.

POP QUIZ

Why are blackberry bushes so common in Seattle?
ⓐ They grow very quickly and are hard to get rid of.
ⓑ People plant the bushes in their gardens.

KEY WORDS

- lots of
- thorny
- blackberry
- cover
- get rid of (= remove)

- thorn
- sharp
- steep
- fortunately
- move around

- stem
- in charge of
- rent

This is a treat for the goats, which don't mind the sharp thorns as they swallow the stems, and it is a great help to the city. Most of the people who live in the city don't even know that the goats are helping them so much!

KEY WORDS

- treat

- swallow

Raising Children

Sometimes, animals step in to do a job that should be done by a human, but the human has failed to do it properly. There is a famous book by Rudyard Kipling called *The Jungle Book*. In it, a boy called Mowgli is lost in the jungle. He is found by a black panther and taken to a wolf family, where he is raised with the wolf cubs. This is only fiction, and you may think that this would not happen in real life. But there are many stories of animals raising human children who have no parents.

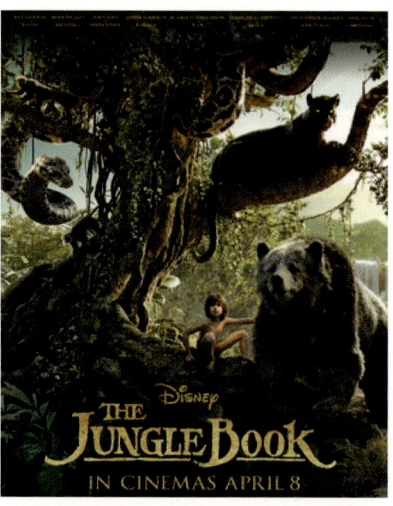

▲ *The Jungle Book* movie poster, directed and produced by Jon Favreau, released in 2016

POP QUIZ

What found Mowgli in *The Jungle Book*?

ⓐ a wolf family
ⓑ a black panther

KEY WORDS

- step in
- fail
- panther
- fiction
- pack
- garbage can
- predator
- female

In 2001, a ten-year-old boy was discovered in Chile, living in a cave with a pack of wild dogs. The boy had suffered a difficult childhood and had not been well cared for by his parents. When another home was found for him, he didn't like it, and he ran away. Then, he disappeared into the wild and lived for two years with the wild dogs. The dogs showed him how to hunt for food in garbage cans, and protected him from predators. The people who found the boy think that he drank milk from the female dogs, like a puppy.

The boy was named "Dogboy" by the media. He was not happy when he was taken from the dogs and brought back to live with humans.

"The dogs are my family," he told police officers. "Please let me go back to them."

He even jumped into the icy waters of the sea to try to escape and to go back to the dogs. But a police officer dived in after him and brought him back to shore. The boy was becoming ill because he was not getting the right food, so he could not stay with the dogs. After a night in hospital, he was taken to a new home to be cared for by people.

Another boy, Andrei Tolstyk, was raised by a single dog in Siberia. When the boy was three months old, his mother left the family home and Andrei was looked after by his father.

Sadly, the father had problems of his own and could not look after the boy properly, so he abandoned Andrei soon afterwards.

KEY WORDS

- media
- icy
- escape
- look after
- of one's own
- abandon
- feral
- on all fours
- social worker
- sign language
- make one's (own) bed

Until the age of seven, Andrei was cared for in the wild by a feral dog, which taught him to walk on all fours, sniff his food before he ate it, and to be aggressive toward humans. When he was found by social workers, Andrei was afraid of people, and tried to bite them. But he was taken to a safe home, where adults managed to speak to him using sign language. After two weeks in his new home, Andrei was walking on two legs like any other human. He also learned to use a spoon, make his own bed, and catch a ball in his hands.

Three years earlier, in Argentina, a one-year-old boy was cared for by eight cats that lived on the streets. The boy and his father were homeless, and one day the boy wandered away. His father was looking for pieces of cardboard to sell in order to make some money to buy food. He did not know where the boy had gone. For several days, cats looked after the little boy. They kept him warm on freezing nights by lying on top of him. The cats tried to clean the boy by licking dried mud from his skin, and they brought him scraps of food to eat. A police woman found the boy, but when she tried to take him from the cats, they protected him by spitting at her and trying to scratch her. The brave police woman managed to pick up the boy and then she took him back to his father.

POP QUIZ

In Argentina, why did the homeless boy's father want cardboard?

ⓐ He wanted to sell it.
ⓑ He wanted to make a shelter with it.

KEY WORDS

- homeless
- cardboard
- mud

- **scrap** (*cf*. scraps)
- **spit** (spit-spitted/spat-spitted/spat)

Scientific Research

Some animals help scientists with their research by going to secret places that humans cannot reach. One of the greatest problems facing humans today is climate change. Climate change can cause extreme weather. This weather can cause floods, fires, or other disasters that threaten the lives of humans and animals. Scientists need to collect data in order to find out what is happening to the planet. But sometimes this data can be difficult to collect. One thing that they need to do is to monitor the temperature of the oceans all over the planet. This tells them if the oceans are getting warmer.

▲ arctic ice melting due to global warming

KEY WORDS

- research
- climate
- extreme weather (*cf.* extreme)

- flood
- threaten
- collect

- data (*cf.* datum)
- monitor

The ocean off Greenland is cold and is filled with pieces of ice. It is much too cold for humans to dive in.  So scientists are using narwhals to help them with their research. A narwhal

▲ narwhal

is a small whale with a large tusk(a type of long, thin tooth). Narwhals naturally live in the icy ocean, and can dive down to a depth of more than a mile.

POP QUIZ
Why can't humans dive in the ocean off Greenland?
ⓐ The water is too polluted.
ⓑ The water is too cold.

KEY WORDS

- be filled with
- narwhal
- tusk
- naturally
- depth

Scientists have attached thermometers and satellite transmitters to a group of narwhals. The temperature data is sent back to the surface, where the scientists can look at them on their computers. This means that they can accurately measure the temperature at different depths below the surface. By doing

▲ sea lion

this, they have found that the ocean is even warmer than they

▲ seal

expected.  Seals, sea lions, and dolphins have also been used to collect data from the oceans.

POP QUIZ

What is sent back to the surface from the narwhals?
ⓐ seals and sea lions
ⓑ temperature data

KEY WORDS

- attach
- thermometer
- satellite transmitter

- accurately
- expect
- seal

- sea lion

Finding Land Mines

In some parts of the world where there have been wars, there are land mines hidden in the ground. They have never exploded, so they are very dangerous. They can explode when a human or a heavy animal steps on them. This can cause terrible injuries or death, and it is dangerous for a human to look for these land mines in order to make them safe. The problem is that nobody knows where they are, so humans need animals to find these hidden killers.

Two animals that can safely help with this difficult task are rats and bees. African pouched rats have been trained to find land mines by their sense of smell. They are too light to make the land mines explode, so they are not in danger.

Bees are difficult to train, but by observing their behavior closely, scientists have found that they can detect where land mines are. The bees are safe because they are very light and rarely land on the mine, preferring to stay in the air.

Bees are very sensitive to different odors. They are attracted to flowers that have a strong scent. This means that they are also good at detecting the chemical odor that comes from a hidden land mine.

Scientists have noticed that when a bee smells this odor, it makes a special buzzing sound, which is different from its usual buzz. Scientists can use this information to make a map of where the land mines are. This helps people to avoid them or to remove them safely. It is possible that scientists may use bees to detect different kinds of pollution or chemical weapons.

KEY WORDS

- land mine
- step on
- terrible
- death
- look for

- killer
- African pouched rat
- observe
- rarely
- prefer

- attract
- buzzing (*cf.* buzz)
- avoid
- pollution
- weapon

Hunting

Animals have been used for thousands of years to help humans hunt for both food and sport. Birds of prey, such as hawks and falcons, are predators of small animals such as small birds or rabbits. ⚗(Aha!) These birds' natural behavior can be used by humans to hunt small animals in order to eat them.

Hunting with birds was especially popular in Europe in the 13th~17th centuries, and falconry is still considered a sport today. The bird is carried on the arm of the handler, who wears a thick leather glove. This protects the handler's skin from the bird's sharp claws and beak. A strip of leather is attached to a leg of the bird to prevent it from flying away until the command is given by the handler.

KEY WORDS

- for sport
- bird of prey (*cf.* prey)
- hawk
- falcon
- popular

- century
- falconry
- consider
- leather
- claw

- beak
- strip
- command

Sometimes the bird wears a leather hood over its eyes.
This keeps it calm and relaxed until it is time to fly. When the
handler gives the command and releases the bird, it is free
to fly where it chooses. This can be quite a risky moment for
the handler. The bird may choose to fly away completely! But
the bird knows that it will be rewarded with a piece of meat if it
returns to the handler, so it does not usually fly far away.

KEY WORDS

- **hood**
- **choose** (choose-chose-chosen)

- **risky** (= dangerous)
- **completely**

When falconry was used to hunt for food, the bird would bring back its prey to the handler. In modern times, falconry is carried out for display purposes, or for the pleasure of handling a wild bird and seeing its power.

▲ cormorant

Fishermen in parts of Asia use birds called cormorants to help them to catch fish. This is often done as a display for tourists rather than to catch food. But some fishermen still feed their families in this way. A cormorant naturally dives for fish to feed itself. Clever fishermen have trained the birds to dive for fish to feed them instead. The cormorants are tamed when they are young, so that they trust the fishermen.

KEY WORDS

- modern times
- display
- purpose
- pleasure

- fishermen
- cormorant
- tame
- trust

- take out
- shaped
- fit

When they are ready to work, the cormorants are taken out on a fishing boat. Collars shaped like rings are fitted to their necks and attached to a rope. The cormorants wear the collars so that they cannot swallow any big fish, although they can swallow smaller ones.

POP QUIZ

Where is the rope attached to a fishing cormorant?

ⓐ to a chain around its foot
ⓑ to a collar around its neck

Without the collars, the birds would eat all the fish they catch!
The cormorants dive to catch fish, and the fishermen guide
them back to the boat. They take the fish from the cormorants,
and keep them. When the cormorants have caught enough fish
for their handlers, the collar is removed. Then, they are free to
catch and eat as many fish as they like.

We have seen that there are many ways in which animals help humans. Sometimes the animals are specially trained to help, but sometimes they *choose* to help in times of danger or need. These events show that animals make strong relationships with humans, and that they can understand when a human is in need. These animals show intelligence, courage, and loyalty. There are many humans all over the world who owe their lives, their health, or their happiness to amazing animals in action.

POP QUIZ

What is the main reason that animals help humans?
ⓐ They are afraid of humans.
ⓑ They make strong relationships with humans.

KEY WORDS

- make a relationship with
- in need
- intelligence
- loyalty
- owe

Comprehension Quiz

A Fill in each blank with the right word below to complete each sentence.

licking	lying	spitting

❶ The cats kept the boy warm by _____ on top of him.

❷ The cats tried to clean the boy by _____ him.

❸ The cats protected the boy by _____ at the police woman.

B Choose the best answer to each question.

❶ Why didn't the police let Dogboy go back to his dog family?

a) He was becoming ill.

b) He was unhappy with the dogs.

c) He was not getting any food.

d) He was not safe with the dogs.

❷ Why does the cormorant wear a collar around its neck?

a) to look attractive

b) to help it to dive deeper

c) to stop it swallowing big fish

d) to stop it swallowing any fish at all

C Solve the crossword puzzle.

Across ❸ The ability to think is called i_____.

Down ❶ Another word for bravery is c_____.

❷ If your body is well, then you are in good h_____.

❹ To stay by someone's side, no matter what happens, is to show l_____.

Let's Review the Story

Fill in the blanks to review the story.

Title: _____

Chapter 1: Incredible Rescues

- A _____ saved its owner from a cow.
- Lions saved a girl from k_____ .
- D_____ saved swimmers from a s_____ .
- A whale saved a _____ from drowning.
- A _____ saved a boy from other g_____ .
- Elephants saved children from a t_____ .

Chapter 2: Catching Criminals

- A parrot solved a m_____ in India.
- Dogs are trained to sniff for d_____ , e_____ , and fruit.
- Cat h_____ solved the murder of Lori Auker.
- Forensic scientists use b_____ to determine when a person _____ .

Chapter 3: Health Heroes

- A p_____ saved its owner from a h_____ attack.
- A r_____ saved its owner from diabetes.
- D_____ can detect cancer by smelling the c_____ in people's breath.
- G_____ dogs or horses help people who are b_____ to find their way around.

Chapter 4: Secret Supporters

- B_____ carry p_____ from one plant to another, and l_____ eat aphids.
- G_____ eat b_____ bushes on the steep hills of Seattle.
- N_____ help scientists to collect d_____ about the temperature of the ocean.
- C_____ help fishermen to catch f_____ in Asia.

Let's Think & Talk

Think about the following questions and answer them freely.

❶ In the book, which story impressed you the most? Why?

❷ Have you ever got any help from animals or been comforted by them? Tell your friends about your experience with animals.

❸ What is your favorite animal? Explain to your friends why you like it, what characteristics it has, how it helps you, etc.

❹ If you know any animals with remarkable activities or peculiar characteristics, share the story with your friends.

Answers

Title: Animals in Action

Chapter 1: Incredible Rescues

- A horse saved its owner from a cow.
- Lions saved a girl from kidnappers .
- Dolphins saved swimmers from a
  shark .
- A whale saved a diver from
  drowning.
- A gorilla saved a boy from other
  gorillas .
- Elephants saved children from a
  tsunami .

Chapter 2: Catching Criminals

- A parrot solved a murder in India.
- Dogs are trained to sniff for drugs ,
  explosives , and fruit.
- Cat hairs solved the murder of
  Lori Auker.
- Forensic scientists use bugs to
  determine when a person died .

Chapter 3: Health Heroes

- A pig saved its owner from a
  heart attack.
- A rabbit saved its owner from
  diabetes.
- Dogs can detect cancer by smelling
  the chemicals in people's breath.
- Guide dogs or horses help people
  who are blind to find their way
  around.

Chapter 4: Secret Supporters

- Bees carry pollen from one
  plant to another, and ladybugs eat
  aphids.
- Goats eat blackberry bushes on
  the steep hills of Seattle.
- Narwhals help scientists to collect
  data about the temperature of the
  ocean.
- Cormorants help fishermen to
  catch fish in Asia.

Smart Readers: **Wise** & **Wide**

After-reading Test

- Animals in Action
- Level 6
- 28 Questions

(Vocabulary 6 / Reading Comprehension 16 /

Sentence Structure & Grammar 6)

Animals in Action After-reading Test

1. What does "venom" mean in the following sentence?

A rattlesnake is known for its powerful venom.

① bite   ② tail

③ poison   ④ strength

2. What does "tsunami" mean in the following sentence?

The 2004 earthquake caused a tsunami.

① a fire caused by an earthquake

② a wave that is big enough to destroy buildings

③ a cyclone that occurs after a thunderstorm

④ a shipwreck that happens due to large waves

3. What does "adrenaline" mean in the following sentence?

The gerbils were trained to press a lever if they detected the odor of adrenaline in the air.

① another name for sweat

② a chemical produced in the human body

③ an explosive chemical

④ the odor of aircraft fuel

4. What does "narwhal" mean in the following sentence?

> Scientists are using <u>narwhals</u> to help them with their research.

① a satellite transmitter ② a type of whale
③ a thermometer ④ an ocean current

※ Choose the right word for each blank. (5~6)

5.
> Perhaps it's not surprising that _____ animals will protect their owners in situations of danger.

① wild ② constant
③ forensic ④ domestic

6.
> Epilepsy is a problem with the brain, which can cause people to have a _____.

① seizure ② autism
③ diabetes ④ tumor

7. How did Zoey protect Booker from the rattlesnake? Choose *two* answers.
① She bit it and it died.
② She placed herself between it and Booker.
③ She barked for help.
④ She chased it away.

8. When might dolphins be aggressive toward humans?
   ① when humans come near them in boats
   ② when sharks are nearby
   ③ when dolphins have babies with them
   ④ when humans swim in the water

9. Why did the boy in India run into the hut when the wave approached?
   ① He knew that it would be safer there.
   ② He thought that the rest of his family were in there.
   ③ He panicked and did not think carefully.
   ④ He went in to rescue his dog from the wave.

10. How did the dog save the boy from the tsunami? Choose *two* answers.
    ① The dog grabbed the boy by the collar of his shirt.
    ② The dog ran uphill and hoped that the boy would follow.
    ③ The dog stood in the doorway of the hut so that the boy could not go in.
    ④ The dog nipped at the boy's heels and nudged him to make him run up
       the hill.

11. What do Jordan's Royal Desert Forces use camels for? Choose *two* answers.
    ① gathering together wild animals in desert
    ② catching smugglers
    ③ keeping crowds in order at soccer matches
    ④ recovering stolen cars from the rough terrain

12. Why are travelers NOT allowed to bring fruit into Australia?
   ① The Australians want travelers to buy their fruit.
   ② The fruit goes rotten on the long journey to Australia.
   ③ The fruit may carry pests and diseases that would harm Australian fruit trees.
   ④ The fruit may be poisonous to humans.

13. Why are dogs trained to sit down when they find an explosive device?
   ① to make sure that the device does not explode
   ② to make sure that nobody knows it has been found
   ③ to allow the handler time to think about what to do
   ④ to encourage people to stay calm

14. How do forensic scientists use bugs to find out when a person died?
   ① The scientists measure the size of the larvae.
   ② The scientists count how many flies are on the cadaver.
   ③ The scientists count how many eggs are on the cadaver.
   ④ The scientists work out where the bugs came from.

15. Which of these is NOT the thing that Lulu did?
   ① She dragged Jo Ann outside.
   ② She managed to open the gate.
   ③ She waited for a gap in the traffic.
   ④ She lay down on the highway.

16. If a dog knows that a child is going to have a seizure, how does it help?
    ① It moves the furniture out of the way.
    ② It places itself so that the child can fall on it safely.
    ③ It licks the child's lips.
    ④ It runs to fetch an adult.

17. Which of these things can an assistance dog NOT do?
    ① go shopping
    ② remove laundry from the washing machine
    ③ pick up items from the floor
    ④ prepare a meal

18. How does stroking a pet help a person's health?
    ① The person's blood pressure drops and they feel relaxed.
    ② The person becomes less allergic to animals.
    ③ The person's blood sugar level remains the same.
    ④ The person can breathe more easily.

19. How does it help plants when bees take pollen from one plant to another?
    ① It allows the plants to grow taller.
    ② It allows the plants to produce fruit and seeds.
    ③ It allows the plants to control pests.
    ④ It allows the plants to make more leaves.

20. How did Dogboy try to escape from the police?
   ① He climbed a tall building.
   ② He jumped into the sea.
   ③ He stole a car and drove away.
   ④ He ran away from a hospital.

21. Why do scientists need to monitor the temperature of the oceans?
   ① to find out the best place for humans to swim
   ② to find out the best place for narwhals to swim
   ③ to find out how quickly the world's climate is changing
   ④ to find out how deep the oceans are

22. How do scientists know when a bee has detected the odor of a land mine?
   ① It flies in a different way.
   ② It lands on the ground in a different way.
   ③ It feeds in a different way.
   ④ It buzzes in a different way.

※ Choose the wrong part of each sentence. (23~24)

23.
   Scratching at an explosive device may cause it explode.
   ①   ②   ③   ④

24.

> It is <u>many</u> <u>too</u> cold <u>for</u> humans <u>to</u> dive in.
>   ①   ②   ③   ④

※ Choose the correct word(s) for each blank. (25~26)

25.

> Other children may have a health problem with their thoughts and feelings _____ in their body.

① than

② but

③ rather than

④ more than

26.

> By doing this, they have found that the ocean is _____ warmer than they expected.

① too

② most

③ as

④ even

※ Choose the correct sentence. (27~28)

27. ① If she have been alone, she would certainly have died of hypothermia.

② If she have been alone, she would certainly had died of hypothermia.

③ If she had been alone, she would certainly have died of hypothermia.

④ If she had been alone, she would certainly die of hypothermia.

28. ① The dog enjoys it as if it is a game.

② The dog enjoys it as if it are a game.

③ The dog enjoys it as if it was a game.

④ The dog enjoys it as if it were a game.

Memo

Memo

Sarah J. Dodd

Sarah J. Dodd is an experienced primary school teacher who resides in the UK, but has also lived and taught in Australia. She has a PhD in Science and a certificate in Creative Writing. She has published several books for children: "An Angel Anyway" (Anyway Press, 2008) the "Little Angels" series (Lion Children's Books, 2009/10), "The Lion Picture Bible" (Lion Children's Books, 2015) and "Legs: the tale of a meerkat lost and found" (Lion Children's Books, 2015). Her poetry for children has also been highly commended and published in the anthology "Let in the Stars" (Manchester Metropolitan University, 2014).

She is currently working on further picture books for the very young, and a novel for older children.

Animals in Action

Written by Sarah J. Dodd
Illustrated by Hyeyeong Kim

First Published in October 2016

Editorial Manager: Juyon Choi
Editors: Juyon Choi, Hyunjeong Kim, Kyunghee Jang, Jiyeong Park
Designer: Eunhee Lee
Cover Designer: Eunhee Lee

Published and distributed by

Darakwon Bldg., 64-1 Jandari-ro, Mapo-gu, Seoul, Korea 04031
Tel: 82-2-736-2031(ext. 250)   Fax: 82-2-732-2037
Homepage: www.ihappyhouse.co.kr
Publisher: Kyudo Chung

ISBN: 978-89-6653-414-2 18740 / 978-89-6653-156-1 18740(set)

[Components]
• 1 Audio CD (Recording Studio: Aram)
• Answer Keys & Korean Translation: Free download at www.ihappyhouse.co.kr